GAIUS VALERIUS CATULLUS

Complete Poetic Works

Translated by Jacob Rabinowitz

SPRING PUBLICATIONS
THOMPSON, CONN.

Published by Spring Publications
Thompson, Conn.
www.springpublications.com

Second, revised edition 2023 (2.0)

First published in 1991

Cover image:

Sleeping Faun
First Century B.C.E.
Bronze
National Archaeological Museum of Naples

ISBN: 978-0-88214-151-0

Library of Congress Control Number: 2023945784

Dedicated to

William H. Clark
my high school Latin teacher
if only you had lived to see how much I learned from you

Contents

Acknowledgments 7

Preface 9

The Poems

Friends 17

Lesbia 55

Rivals for Lesbia 69

Juventius 87

Bithynia 97

Brother Death 105

Politics 119

Mythological Poetry 129

Concordance 163

Acknowledgments

I thank Elli Mylonas for her time and cheerful expertise in teaching me the use of the computer by which this manuscript was prepared. Also, she created beautiful and intelligential *macros,* which brought sudden order to many a disparate file. Eliel Mamousette also deserves praise for his timely aid computer-wise.

Prof. Charles Boer of the University of Connecticut has made valuable suggestions from which the work has taken new luster. *Gratias ago.*

I also thank my friends Peter Wilson, Brett Rutherford, George Scrivani, and Frederic Evans for their aid, criticism and patience.

I am finally and decisively indebted to Jay Livernois, this work's advocate and champion, through whom it reached the right hands at the right time.

Any error or oversight in this book is, of course, mine and mine alone.

Preface

I

Who Is This Cat?

Catullus's poetry crackles and flashes with a desperate energy, almost as if he sensed how short his life would be. Above all a lover, his greatest erotic verses take their keenness from the feeling that it can't wait (39–5); Orcus, the ugly shadow (44–3), is already tapping his shoulder with a long cold finger; ecstasy is a furtive thing (41–7) to be elegantly filched from the pocket of Time.

For this reason there is a note of foreboding in all his treatments of love —and his favorite scenes are departures and desertions. The whole Lesbia cycle revolves around defection and betrayal. In the insult poems Catullus's sense of existence as endangered comes out in the character of the abuse. His assailants are monsters of appetite. A man who scents his girlfriend (5–13) may turn into a giant nose and literally snuff her up. A guest, on sighting Catullus's fine furnishings (37–25), whirls them out of the house in a hurricane of kleptomania.

Taken together, the poems create a portrait of a man who feels his being ever escaping, the loss as frightening as that of blood would be. He hears the hot drops falling and searches for the wound.

As if a dying man, Catullus has nothing to lose. The time to live, the time to love is *now.* He has no use for abstractions, religious, political, or moral. Duty, the hobgoblin of Roman minds, seems to him a plaything of delirium. He has the contempt for authority native to Anarchists and Bushmen. He richly squanders everything but time.

His insults make one hilarious ruin of gangsters, generals, and bath-house boys. He havocs the lot in transports of dandyism militant. With an indifference to consequence that may account for his early and unexplained death, he trounces the consensus morality of the sour, pleasure—hating Romans—a nation of soldiers and lawyers, whom his Grecian refinement would have struck as faggy and subversive in equal degrees. Had this prince of insolence survived into Augustus's reign of repression, theres little doubt he would have faced death or exile.

Born about 84 B.C., dying before he was thirty, Catullus came of wealthy North-Italian landowners, grew up in Verona and moved to Rome in his late teens.

Before him, Roman literature was a wasteland. Epics that read like recruiting posters and lumbering, low class comedies. The Romans were yokels—and knew it. They'd do anything to feel less boorish and stupid around the Greeks. Rather like the Americans felt about the British in the nineteenth century. Now Catullus took his cues from Sappho and Archilochus among the ancients and could blandly assume their styles, along with those of Theocritus, Callimachus and Apollonius of Rhodes, those Hellenistic masters with whom Greek poetry had splendidly trembled and elegantly died in the third century B.C.E.—two hundred years before Catullus. In his mastery of their modes Catullus could be likened to a brilliant Jazz musician equally proficient in nineteenth-century style symphonies.

With this achievement Catullus transformed Roman literature from a military camp to an elegant suburb of Alexandria. Vergil, Horace, Ovid—all the Latins after—studied Catullus as a sure-fire guide.

For me and mine, who've come to loathe the lying abstractions of politics and religion, Catullus is a hero. He has our need to live vividly, to invent oneself, to be legendary. Like us, he "rages greatly, knowing his time is short." From where we stand we're well situated to appreciate the way the Cat made witty gorgeous war on his society. He didn't *have* a cause—he *was* one.

Catullus is one of Academe's best-kept secrets. He's taught in part—usually in expurgated editions—and students are traditionally encouraged to turn their enthusiasm to Horace, a "mature" poet (who sold out eagerly to Augustus and the New Order and wrote exquisite odes advising youths to die in wars of conquest). Catullus is ignored, dismissed as a "young man's interest," and preserved in a Canopic jar, on a back shelf, by a league of tenured dust-buffs. I mean by this book to free the bottled imp—for the same audience who loved him in his lifetime, the noble company of ultra-cool hip and literate *trespassers,* who recognize no boundaries they haven't themselves imagined, for whom boy-whores and subtle verses, elegance and insurrection, mythology and scandal are equal and complementary interests.

II

Rationale of the Translation

I HAVE tried to present the poems of Catullus in such a way as to simulate the original experience of reading them in Latin, in Catullus's own time. To accomplish this, I have wholly avoided footnotes, finding modern equivalents for ancient things, as saying "the rings under your eyes" where the Roman mark of debauchery was skinny flanks—or using "chicken soup" to represent the Roman cold remedy of nettle broth. Where this anachronistic mode proved awkward, particularly in the case of obscure mythological allusions, I have extended the text.

Glosses and footnotes obscure the poetic effect they aim to clarify. The Latin audience had immediate understanding of the references, and this can be best approximated by providing the information on the spot—in the lines themselves.

But in all I have been strictly faithful to the spirit and sense of the text. I have neither added nor subtracted, but imaginatively delivered, what was there. No mistaken shame has made me muffle Catullus's sexual directness, and I have never exceeded the freedom of the Latin.

I have used Kenneth Quinn's edition, departing from it occasionally to favor the *Oxford Classical Text* of Mynors: at (traditional numeration) 25.5, which Mynors obelizes, I read with some editors of the Latin text *diva mulier,* 36.10 *iocose,* 62.9 *vincere,* 64.11 *prima...Amphitriten,* 64.14 *freti,* 77.11 *horribile aequor,* 90.5 *gratus,* 98.8 *abstersisti omnibus,* 115.5 *saltusque paludesque.* Mynors also supplies the fragments.

Conflations and separations of the text are indicated. I have in a few places divided the text into several voices, in 30-45 purely for vividness, otherwise where clarity and clear author—intent demanded, as in the choral poems.

Untranslatable puns and witticisms required more boldness, and 83-24, 85-26, 103-93 and 12-84 contain what are really imitations rather than translations. Humor is too volatile for literal transfer, and greater accuracy would have turned Catullus from a wit to a pedant.

My rendering of the mini-epic 116-64 cuts some of the elaboration. The Greeks, and particularly the Romans, prized a rather florid oratoric style, which in English comes off as frigid bombast. Our epic heritage is rooted in the terse, hard-hitting Anglo Saxon. Hence the poems had to be aligned with a different tradition to keep the epic flavor, which meant some re-forging, especially in the speeches. Yet the burden of the lines is preserved scrupulously, and nothing in the original but is indicated or suggested in my re-write.

The order of the poems is my own—a roughly categorical or thematic arrangement. The manuscript and, following it, all previous translations have ordered the verses according to the meters employed. The effect is unintelligibility, pure randomness. When Catullus died he had not (by my reading) put the final hand to many of the poems—some were merely epigrams he may never have intended to publish—much less arranged in order. Thus a re-ordering of the poems, so as to follow his development of themes and portraits, seemed desirable. The numbers at the head of each poem are, first, that of its place in this arrangement, then the traditional numeration of the Latin manuscript. Poems 18, 19, and 20, universally acknowledged to be spurious—and, what is worse, uninteresting—are omitted.

Where anything helpful is known about the persons mentioned in the text, I have briefly related the pertinent. Most are now only names. Throughout, my source for biographical notes has been Chester Louis Neudling's *A Prosopography to Catullus* (Oxford, 1955).

I hope this book will be used by students of the classics to clarify and challenge their sense of the author's tone and intent. For the more general reader and amateur of antiquity, it provides easy and I hope agreeable access to the time and the man.

For those who have not read him in Latin, I assure you that the original poems are, every one, rich and rare. Any flaw, hair, or crack in these translations should be attributed not to Catullus but to his unworthy servant and yours,

Jacob Rabinowitz

The Poems

1–1

Cornelius Nepos, historian, about ten years older than Catullus, may have been his patron or guardian when he got to Rome. Like Catullus, he was a North Italian.

To WHOM shall I dedicate my new little book, a fresh
papyrus roll, the edges rubbed smooth with
pumice-stone?
To you, Nepos, because you used to think my nonsense
was worth your listening,
even though you'd already published your history of the
world where you, alone of the Italians,
dared set forth all time in one volume of learned and—
Jupiter!—painstaking pages.
So, it's yours, the whole of my book, such as it is.
O Virgin Protectress, Muse of Lyric Poetry,
let it last, and remain to be read by another generation.

2–14*b*

...IF YOU read through these poor scribblings
of mine,
if you're not too dainty to touch my book...

Friends

CATULLUS, fucketeer playboy in the midst of a collapsing republic, was a poet—roughly the Roman equivalent of a rock star. He could terrify a general or win a woman (or boy) just by inviting him or her to be the hero of a poem. Caesar begged for his friendship, and, what's more remarkable, Cicero shut up when he spoke. He was like royalty-poet-prince of the world's capital.

3-27

HAVE the wine-cellar slave bring in something stronger,
mix us some really relentless cups. Postumia demands
it, mistress of the feast, fuller of wine than a grape!
Don't come near me with that waterjug—let ultra-
conservative old-Roman types weaken their wine.
We'll drink it straight up. Hey slave, another cup of
undiluted Bacchus! I'll have nothing in my glass but
the god!

4-102

A note to Cornelius Nepos, requesting gossip

IF ANYONE ever received a confidence with trusty silence
and as a friend, Cornelius,
if anyone was known for his deep honesty,
you'll find in me one initiate into the mysteries of
discretion,
you'd think I'd turned into Harpocrates, god of Quiet,
whose finger is ever at his lips.

5–13

FABULLUS, you'll dine well at my home a few days from
now, the gods willing,
just remember to bring all the courses, dessert, wine,
a pretty girl, don't forget the salt—
and do try to be amusing!
Bring all that along and you'll have a great meal.
My wallet, you see, is full of cobwebs—
But, in return, I'm serving up my undiluted affection,
and something more agreeable and refined than that:
I'll let you sniff that fragrance my girl gives off when
she's possessed by the god of Love—
when you smell it, you'll beg the gods to turn you into
a great big nose.

6–49

Cicero was an upholder of "good old-fashioned" Roman poetry, and this may have led to some friction between him and Catullus.

MY DEAR, clear-spoken Cicero, most eloquent of all the
descendants of Romulus
that were, are, or will be:
Catullus offers you his profoundest thanks.
"And how great are those thanks, Catullus?"
They're deep as the hell where bad poets go,
and high as the scintillant summits of your lawyerly glory.

17

COLONIA, I know you want to have a festival procession
along that long bridge of yours. You're all set to go
bounding over it—
but the bridge shakes in apprehension on its bandylegged
trestles
patched and propped with odd lumber scraps.
It's afraid of falling back-flat into deep swamp.

I personally hope your bridge'll be so good to you it could
even stand up to the priests of Mars
hopping and howling the war dance all across it.
—In return for these good wishes of mine, I'd like, as
a favor, a good laugh.

Could it be arranged for one of my fellow-citizens to slip
from the bridge, sail over the side and head first under
the mud
at the deepest point in that whole semiliquid lake
where the rotting marsh achieves its richest shade
of oily blue-black?
The guy's a jerk. He's about as knowing as a two-year-old
asleep in his father's rocking arms.
Now he's married a young girl, a glory of innocent
freshness, a flower,
a girl as daintysoft as a baby goat,
a girl deserving more painstaking protection than the rich
dark grapes perfecting on the vine.

Yet he lets her play where she pleases, he doesn't care,
    doesn't bestir himself
any more than an axe-hacked hunk of log
halfsunk in a greenmantled standing pool.
The numbskull sees, hears nothing, doesn't know what,
    or if, he is.
So shake him out of that dullness, pitch him off,
    O bridge,
have him leave his former sluggish life behind in that
    thick slime
as a mule might lose its iron shoe in sucking mud.

8–55 *&* 58*b*

CAMERIUS, if it isn't too much trouble, I'd really like to
know where you're hiding out these days.
I looked for you at the racetrack, the bookstores, Jupiter's
temple, Pompey's theater—
I stopped all the girls, demanded your whereabouts—they
denied any knowledge, faces calm with innocence.
I wasn't satisfied. "You tramps, I pressed, "where's
Camerius? I know you know!"
One of them opened her blouse and said:
"Here he is, hiding between my tits!"
Camerius, old buddy, being your friend is a labor of
Hercules.

If I were Talus, the giant bronze robot Vulcan constructed
as guardian of Crete,
who patrolled the island with ten-mile strides,
if I could fly, like Pegasus, across the ground and gallop
through the air,
if I were an Olympic footrace victor, or wore, like Perseus,
Mercury's winged shoes,
if I were the white racing team Ulysses and Domed stole
from king Rhesus,
if I were all the birds of the air and every wind at once—
I'd still end up exhausted, bones a total ache, from the
way I have to hunt for you.

You know, it's tremendously arrogant of you to deny
yourself to me—
Where are you! Tell it, speak out! Has some girl got you
under lock and key?
Clam up, will you? Throw away my love like it was
nothing?
Don't you know, my silent friend, that Venus, ruler of
affection,
rejoices in talk? Look, don't tell me if you don't want to—
it's not that important. But give me *some* assurance you
really are my friend.

9-12

ASINIUS Marrucinus, can't you just have a few drinks, a
few laughs, without your hands getting into trouble?
Not to put too fine a point on it—you pocket your
napkin when the host isn't looking.
You think it's cute? It's low.
Clod! You have no idea how *inelegant*, how *shabby*—
Don't believe me? Believe your brother Pollio. He'd pay
any sum to stop your pilfering.
Pollio knows what's charming or amusing—and what isn't.
Either give me back my napkin, or plan on being the hero
of a poem:
—not that I really care about the *napkin*, but my friends
Fabullus and Veranus
sent me the set of good flax table linen from Spain, where
they're stationed.
My friends, understand? The friends I love.

10–112

You'RE one of the great ones, Naso—
and yet there aren't a great many men
who want to be seen strolling with you.
Your eminence
has never been questioned. You're a great
bore, and a great one for taking it up the ass.

11–98

CRUDDY Victius, you make me understand what people
mean when they use terms like "sewer-mouth,
or "a tongue to wipe your shoes on."
Your big stupid yap makes it all come alive.
Why don't I go to hell?
Hey, I'm listening to you—isn't that enough?

12–50

Calvus (Gaius Licinius Calvus Macer) was a poet, orator, and lawyer-colleague of Cicero's; his epigrams stung both Caesar and Pompey.

YESTERDAY, Licinius, we made a leisurely game of writing
verses in turn, then lines in reply.
(A pastime befitting sensitive gentlemen.)
We varied the meters with the changes of theme to see
who could use them most ingeniously—
replying to each other as we tippled and laughed.
I left there, Licinius, all fired up with your playful wit,
your sense of the elegant—
so much so that I hadn't any appetite, sleep couldn't close
my eyes on a dream, I tossed and turned all over
the bed
excited! Crazily waiting for day so I could be with you,
talk to you!
When I finally got my exhausted self stretched out
half-dead,
I made this poem for you, delightful man. See how
I suffer!
Don't rashly ignore my entreaties for another such visit,
darling friend.
Remember Nemesis, who takes revenge on those who
scorn others' love.
See to it you don't offend that powerful, touchy goddess.

13-96

To Calvus, on the death of Calvus's wife

IF THE dead take any pleasure in our grief, if the tomb is
silently grateful for our tears—
for the pained way we recall old passions and friendship
lost—
then your wife Quintilia's early death is not so much
a hurt
as your love is a joy for her, even in death.

14–53

Vatinius, one of Caesar's tools, used gangster tactics to get political power. When Calvus destroyed him in the mentioned oration, he's supposed to have mopped his sweating face and shouted to the jury:

"Judges! Must I be condemned just because this man is eloquent?" To which Calvus replied:

"Is it my eloquence that makes you perspire?"

IT WAS great. My friend Calvus was taking Vatinius's guilt
and putting it on display. Stunning.
As you know, Calvus's great stature as a lawyer isn't exactly
in keeping with his height—
Anyway, while Calvus was doing unto Vatinius, this guy
stands up in the spectator section, raising his hands,
all amazed, and goes:
"Great gods, the little prick sure can spout!"

15–14

Calvus, you as a lawyer should know better than to send me such a book.
If you weren't dearer to me than sight, I'd hate you worse than that Vatinius you prosecuted into nothingness.
What did I ever do or say to deserve being drowned in poets? It's death by anthology.
May the gods ruin whatever client gave you this merciless book!
—Unless Sulla, that poor schoolteacher you defended, sent you, in gratitude, this unheard of and ingenious present—
then I don't take it so hard. Quite the contrary! At least you got something for your work.
Great gods! What a horrible, unlucky book you sent your Catullus,
knowing it could kill a man in twenty-four hours,
and just before the Saturnalia, my favorite holiday!

No, no, my witty friend, I'm not letting you off so easy.
At daybreak (if the dawn ever comes) I'm running to the bookstore,
I'll gather every poison, Scribbilarius, Ennuinius, Suffenus,
—oh, I'll pay you back but good!
And you—bad poets! Drag your lame feet back where you came from.

16–22

Hey Varus, you know that guy Suffenus—he's gracious,
witty, city-slick, and he writes all that poetry?
Lines by the thousand! And not on scrap paper—they're all copied out
on new sheets of the most expensive vellum, bound in leather and stamped with gold.
But if you *read* them, then that lovely gent Suffenus,
the neatest sheet in Rome,
turns into a clod just off the bus from Podunk,
ex-superintendent of goats.
It's quite inconsistent.
The man about town, the *boulevardier,* the smoothest beast in creation,
becomes duller than a suburb the second he starts in with the poetry.
Yet, to see him writing it—it's a vision of human happiness.
He joys in his own existence, his own personality seems to him a delightful surprise—
Well, nobody's so perceptive he isn't Suffenus in something.
No one can see the pack on his own back.

17–35

Go, LETTER, tell my young poetfriend Caecilius he should
leave New Como's walls, abandon Lake Larius's
shore—
and come see me at Verona. I have a few thoughts I'd like
to share with him,
things concerning a certain mutual friend;
if he knew what was up, he'd come at a run, no matter
how many times his dazzling new girlfriend
calls after him, throws her arms around his neck, invoking
Death
that she might not survive his departure.
As I hear it, she's been insane with love ever since she
heard him reading a draft of his *Cybele,*
straightaway passion made the marrow smoulder in
her bones.
Poor learned little girl! I can forgive you for wanting to
keep him at home,
and that *Cybele,* even in rough draft, made an enchanting
poem.

18-56

CATO, old boy, quite the funniest thing—worth your hearing—worth a laugh!
As you love your Catullus, you're sure to snicker at this truly cheerful episode!
Just now in the alley I surprised a little boy shoving it to a girl—
and, may it please Venus! quick as a pistol I shot up his ass.

19–67

Catullus:

Door, ever a pleasure to old Balbus, when the house
was his,
Door, that was always nice to his sweet son Caecilius,
now just married. Door, Jove bless your every hinge!
Everyone had a good word for the way you opened to
Balbus
—tho' the word is you aren't guarding his son very well.
Since the old man was laid to rest and the young heir got
himself married,
you've really let things slide.

Come on, out with it, what's the story behind your
change of heart?
why'd you betray your old loyalty?

Door:

As I wish to please Caecilius who owns me now, I did
nothing wrong—whatever people say!
But whenever folks are angry, they slam the door!
Whatever's wrong, it's the door's fault!

Catullus:

Could you be a little more explicit?

Door:

Can I? No one wants the nuisance of learning about
things they're already sure they know.

Catullus:

I honestly want to know. Don't worry, just tell.

Door:

Well, for a start, that "virgin bride" of Caecilius's was
already married once.
—Not that her first husband ever touched her—
his weak little prick dangled like a rotten carrot.
It never raised its head belt high.
But they say his father broke into the bedroom (a disgrace
to the whole unhappy house),
either because his wicked brains were stewed with lust,
or because his helpless son couldn't plough his own field
and they had to find a prick that packed enough punch to
relieve the girl of her virginity.

Catullus:

A loyal, staunch, upstanding father—who'd piss in his own
son's lap.

Door:

And that's not all. The town of Brixia, by the Cycnean
tower—

Catullus:

Brixia, where the river Mella gently flows,
Brixia, dear mother city of my own Verona!

Door:

—all Brixia's seen that bride screwing the citizens
Postumius and Cornelius.
Now here someone might say:

"How could you know that, door? You never leave
your sill.
Bolted to your frame, you've never traveled further than
you open—how could you hear the town's gossip?"
I've overheard it from the bride herself, often enough,
while she's chatting about her crimes with the maids,
naming the people I mentioned (she never guessed I could
hear and tell)
—also, she mentioned a certain fellow—I won't say who—
he'd throw a tantrum—
but I *can* tell you he's very tall, and he was once hauled
into court on a charge
of fathering some girl's bastard—he got off
when they found out the pregnancy was faked.

20–33

BEST of the bath-house thieves, father Vibenius, you and
your homo son
(greedy, daddy's hands, and greedy the butt of his boy),
why don't you go into exile? Why don't you go to hell?
Everyone knows papa pillages unwatched clothes
and sonny can't make another cent on his hairy ass.

21–38

CORNIFICIUS, your Catullus is sick, dangerously ill and
worse by the hour.
A *word* from you might have been some comfort—but that
was too much to ask.
Is this the return on my affection?
Well, if you want to send me some verses now, don't even
try to cheer me;
send me lines as sad as those Simonides wept
for the Athenians fallen at Marathon.

22–97

So HELP me all the gods, I really don't think it makes
much difference
if you sniff Aemilius's mouth or his ass.
As far as cleanness goes, they're quite the same.

If anything, his ass is neater—and nicer—
since it has no teeth, whereas his mouth
has teeth one and a half feet long
stuck in gums like split wrinkled rawhide,
and when he smiles—
well, did you ever see, on a summer's day, the parted
cunt lips of a pissing mule?

Aemilius has fucked plenty of girls, he thinks he's
really sharp—
yet I can hardly believe he isn't driving
the donkey that turns a mill
—like other not very valuable slaves.

And if any girl could touch him, wouldn't she be the kind
who'd rim a sick executioner?

23-32

O PLEASE, my sweet Ipsitilla, dear delightsome child,
    let me come visit you at noon?
You will? And one other thing—be sure no-one else
    is there. Be sure you're at home, leave the door
    unlocked, get ready
for nine uninterrupted fucks. In fact, why not now?
I just had lunch, I'm lolling here, gorged,
and practically punching a hole through my toga.

24-44

Publius Sestius was a notorious wineswiller and wealthy glutton, whereas Antius, against whom he had written his oration, authored a sumptuary law to forbid unduly luxurious banquets.

I'VE got a little Tiburtine estate—or perhaps I should say
it's in the Sabine hills?
My friends call it a Tiburtine estate, but those who enjoy
my annoyance assert,
at all costs, it's really a farm in the hills.
But, Sabine or, (perhaps) more properly, Tiburtine,
I was glad enough to be in my suburban home
while I got over an awful cough and a bellyache
which my guts gave me as just punishment for chasing
after rich dinners.

I wanted to get an invite from Sestius, so I read through
his oration against Antius,
full of legal poison and sickening lawyer tricks,
then I caught a numbing head cold and a nonstop cough
that shook me half to pieces.
I fled to your lap, my little estate, restored myself with
bed rest and chicken soup.
I'm all better now, and grateful to this place
that granted me compassionate rest
while I was deservedly ill.

Gods, if I ever pick up Sestius's criminal scribblings again,
let chill evening air bring cough and cold
—to Sestius, not me!
To Sestius, who finally invited me to dinner
when my health had been weakened by reading his
awful oration.

25–113

DURING Pompey's first consulship there were two who
enjoyed Maecilia's compliance.
Now that he's re-elected, she still has just two—
thousand.
Adultery's a seed which, in the right soil,
yields fruit even a thousandfold.

26–108

The brothers Gaius and Publius Cominius earned themselves general hatred by prosecuting popular men. Finally they were hurled bodily from the courtroom and had to flee over rooftops to escape a mob.

IF, COMINIUS, you were executed, condemned by
the people,
and you brought your spew-stained white hairs down
to the grave,
I expect that first of all your tongue (perjured to
the tonsils)
would be cut out and thrown to a hungry vulture—
a blackthroated crow would swallow your gouged-out eyes,
the dogs would gulp your guts, the wolves would have
the rest.

27-30

ALFENUS, you cheating ingrate, you're really some tough guy—to whoever was good to you!
You never hesitated to sell me out.
But all the gods in heaven have seen that betrayal comes easy to you,
they all know that when I was down you made my neck a step.
After that, I won't trust anyone.

You coaxed me along, made me think it was safe, waited till I really liked you;
then pulled away. All your promises—words in the wind.

You've already forgotten the whole thing, but the gods remember, and Fides,
goddess of Trust, will find some brutal way
of refreshing your memory.

28-73

DON'T do anyone any favors, never expect loyalty.
Nothing's enough. Kindness does no good.
Look at me: I never found anyone crueler
than the one who said he was my only friend.

29–60

Did a lioness whelp you in the hills of Libya,
or Scylla, whose womb opened and barked
like a mad dog's jaws? Is that where you got
such an ugly, callous mind?

When I was begging for your help, with no one
else to turn to, you treated me
like I was nothing.

Even if you have learned to walk on two legs,
you still have the heart of an animal.

30–45

Septimus held his darling Acme in his lap,
and said:

"If I'm not crazy about you and ready to go on raging
year in and year out,
I hope I become living dinner for a blue-eyed lion
on the singed plains of Libya or India."

Cupid sneezed on the right, then the left: in all,
a lovely omen.

Acme threw back her head with easy grace,
her red lips kissed her sweet boy's lovedrunk eyes.
She said:

"My own little Septikins, sure as looking at you makes
my twat sop,
I hope we never get freed from the slavery of Love!"

Cupid sneezed on the left, then the right: in all,
a lovely omen.

And so they go, the fortunate ones, loved and loving,
soul to soul.

Friends

Says Septimius:
"Caesar can keep his Gaul and Syria, Acme's my kind
of conquest—"
Acme replies:
"All my wishes have just one name: Septimius!"
Who ever saw anyone better off or luckier in love?

31–36

VOLUSIUS's *Rome, An Epic Poem,* fit to be inscribed on toilet paper,
you're about to pay off a vow my girlfriend made. She swore to Venus and Cupid
that, if she ever got me back, and I stopped writing murderous verses against my rivals, shed give a few choice pages
'from those horrid poems' (i.e., mine!) as a truly evil offering
to the lame Firegod.

Nasty little girl! You thought that a real cute thing to promise the gods!
Oceanborn Venus, templed everywhere, I hope you'll consider the score well and wittily settled
—with these *horrid poems.* To the flames, you clunking, ponderous volume,
Volusius's epic poem on Rome—pages worth wiping your ass with.

32–95

MY FRIEND Cinna's poem *Myrrha* was born after nine
winters and harvests had passed,
whereas in one year Hortensius blackened reams of
paper—five hundred thousand lines!
The *Myrrha* will travel as far as Cyprus, where Aphrodite
once played with Myrrha's son Adonis, by the river
Satrachus's curving waves,
the centuries will grow whitehaired unrolling Cinna's scroll
to read that poem again.
While Volusius's *Rome, An Epic Poem* will die at Padua,
the place where it was writ,
its pages will provide leisure suits for mackerels in the
marketplace.
Dear to me are the rare tracks of my friend's pen—
but the public joys in Antimachus's empty bloated books.

33–78

ONE of Gallus's brothers has a lovely son,
the other brother, a delightful wife—
Gallus, pleasant fellow, plays Cupid, so those
two charming young people can lie with one another.
Slick, Gallus is, but clever he isn't;
he shows a nephew how to cuckold an uncle,
forgetting he too's married to someone's pretty aunt...

34–42

I INVOKE the spirit of Satire to make my blood and
being pulse with his pelting rap meters,
God of Mockery, fill me with your force!

There's a rotten slut making a fool out of me, refusing
to return my notebooks filled
with you, O Satire. Is this to be endured?
I'll follow her everywhere, a vengeful pest, demanding
that notebook back.

"Who is she?" you ask. Well, she walks like a tart
and she always has the sickening fixed and phoney grin
of a ham actor—or a French lapdog.

"Rotten slut, my notebook, now! Give it back, you rotten
slut!" I bellow.

"*Note*-book! *Note*-book! Mine! Don't you even care that
I'm out here screaming?"
"You mudpit, you walking whorehouse—and if there's
anything worse than that, you're it!"

That doesn't work. I try plan "B" I shout in such
ironharsh dogshameless
wallshaking tones shell blush that the neighbors can hear.
Louder then, once more:

"Rotten slut, my notebook, now! Give it back,
you rotten slut!"

No good. She doesn't even flinch. Perhaps I should try
a different approach?

"Dear modest lady, my notebook, now! Give it back—
please."

35–110

ONE can speak well of those friendly girls
who get paid for a job well done.
You, Aufilena, promise, and then
you don't put out. Most unfriendly.
To take a fee for services never rendered
is criminal.

It's natural to 'make it' with someone,
it's modest not to. But your half-measures
are neither. In the end you're worse
than a greedy whore whose every hole's
for hire.

36–111

AUFILENA, to live in perfect satisfaction
with a single man is the praise and glory
of a bride. But still, itd be nicer
to sleep with whomsoever,
than to lie with your uncle and hatch your own brothers.

37–25

THALLUS, you faggot, softer than rabbitfur, or goosedown,
or a sweet little earlobe,
or an old man's listless dick, lying in cobwebs and neglect.
—And yet, when the full moon shows the other guests
starting to nod and yawn,
you're grabbier than a plunging hurricane.

Give me back my housecoat, which you *pounced* on,
and my good Spanish flax table napkins, and the painted
boxwood writing tablets,
which you keep on display, jerk, like they were heirlooms,
unstick them from your claws and give them back
or I'll use a whip to scribble some *really* embarrassing lines,
hot as the iron that brands disgrace on a common thief,
on your woolsoft sides and dainty little hands.
You'll get excited in a brand new way, your head will spin
like a boat caught out on the open sea when the winds
go mad.

38-6

WHAT about your new playmate, Flavius? Unless she's
a total dog I don't see how you can help telling.
On the other hand, who knows what kind of hot little
whore turns you on?
One thing's for sure, you're not alone at night. So says
the cologne you started using,
and the crumpled blankets on your flattened mattress,
so says your trembling bed, in a squeak, lurching across
the floor.
Keeping mum can't mask the facts. Look at the bags
under your eyes—
you're all fucked out!

So come on, tell me who it is.
I want to glorify your exploits
in elegant, heavenly verse.

Lesbia

❦

THE Roman conception of the virtuous woman was dreary and strict in the extreme. Decent girls stayed home and did the spinning. Any woman acting differently was a social outcast forever.

A junoesque older woman, sister of a gangster, and a consul's wife, Lesbia broke all the rules for feminine behavior. Imperious, capricious—like Maria Callas, Cleopatra, a female mafiosa—fill in your own *maitresse.*

39-5

THE time to live, the time to love, is now. What our
parents think about it means nothing to us.
It can't wait. Every morning the sun returns to life—
our light is brief as a day, our night is an endless sleep.
Give me a hundred kisses, a thousand, ten thousand,
into the millions, into infinity,
I've got to lose count, lose myself, lose my distrust.
Give me a hundred kisses, a thousand, ten thousand,
if I haven't lost count I know there aren't enough.

40-2

SPARROW, my girl's favorite plaything, she keeps you in
her lap, amused at you,
lets you attack her fingertip, provokes your sharp little nip.
She's the shining center, the glowing focus
of my life. It pleases her to toy with you,
sweet thing, the play-bites distract her
from every sharper pain.

Maybe I could shake this grim feeling I have
if I could play with you as she does—
just forget myself and play.

41-7

You want to know how many kisses would be enough
for me, Lesbia?
The number of sand grains between the tombs of Libya's
ancient lords and the temples where Egypt worships
Jove in the shape of a ram.
The number of stars that watch the furtive
love affairs of humankind
while the night is passing over them in silence.
That's how many would satisfy your crazed Catullus.
What can't be counted can't be an unlucky number.

42-2*b*

On Lesbia's first gentleness to Catullus

...As DEAR to me as the golden apple was
to that rapid girl, Atalanta,
that made her lose the race and her
too long endured virginity.

43-86

QUINTIA is beautiful to many, she has a clear complexion,
she's tall, has good posture—
all points in her favor, individually considered.
But the overall harmony that makes a woman *beautiful*
—ah, no, she hasn't got that elegance, that gracegiving
style.
She's just a big body, compared to Lesbia.

It's as if when Lesbia was perfected, there wasn't enough
charm
left over to adorn the rest of womankind.

44-3

VENUS and Cupid, Spirits of Love,
lament, Desires and Passions mourn;
and all you warmhearted men-about-town.
Weep now, for my girlfriend's sparrow is dead,
her darling bird, more precious to her
than sight. It was sweet, and it knew her
as well as she knew her own mother.

It used to stay right in her lap, hopping
about, here and there, chirping only for its mistress.
Now it goes the black path they say none travel back.

Damn you Orcus, ugly shadow!
You swallow every beautiful thing,
you stole my lovely, delightful bird.
A crime! Poor little sparrow!
My girl's in tears,
her eyes are red and faintly swollen.

45–51

In imitation of a poem by Sappho

HE SEEMS to me a god, even happier than the gods.
He sits with you, sees you, hears your laughter.
It's driving me crazy, 'cause whenever I see you, Lesbia,
I lose control,
my tongue dies in my mouth, subtle heat spreads under
my skin, my ears ring
and I see darkness.

46–72

YOU once said that only Catullus really knew you, Lesbia,
that you'd rather have me than Jupiter—
I loved you, not as an ordinary man loves a woman,
but as a father loves his sons, with patient selflessness.
Now I really *do* know you. While I'm even more ruinously
in love with you, I've learned how worthless you are.
Why do I still love you?
The way you hurt me makes me love you more,
even if it makes me like you less.

47-8

Joyless Catullus, stop playing the fool. Give up what you
see is lost.
Those were your clear seasons, the suns shone frank
and bright, when you used to go wherever your
girlfriend led.
—I loved her. No-one will ever love a girl that much.
You laughed together then, when you were eager and she
wasn't unwilling. White suns shone
openly for you in those clear times.
Now she wants no more of you. Weakling, show her the
same! Don't chase what runs from you, don't live
for sorrow.
Goodbye, girl. Now Catullus is firm. He doesn't need
you, he isn't going to beg.
But you'll be sorry when no-one calls for you. What'll
your life be like? Too bad for you, bitch.
Who'll run after you, think you're beautiful, love you?
Whose girl will you be? When you kiss him will you softly
bite his lip and—
Hey, it's over. Forget about it, Catullus, it's finished.

48–70

My woman says shed rather marry me than anyone,
than Jove himself–
What a woman says to an eager lover
is fit to be inscribed on wind, or running water.

49–83

Lesbia cursed me out–her husband was there–that jerk
was overjoyed to hear it.
Jackass, you don't understand a thing. If she was silent,
it would mean she didn't care
about me. If she growls and bitches, not only am I
on her mind,
but, what's deeper and keener, I make her angry.
She burns for me, and that keeps her talking.

50–104

You really thought I was serious when I was cursing
Lesbia
who is my life, dearer to me than both my eyes?
I couldn't have been in earnest—I love her too much.
—Fools like you believe everything they hear.

51–92

Lesbia's always cursing at me—never shuts up about me.
Damned if she doesn't love me!
What makes me think that? Well, the score is perfectly
even.
I too insult her energetically,
but damned if I don't love her.

52–75

IT'S gotten to the point, Lesbia, where my mind is so
totally wasted,
ruined, by your whorishness and my own devotion
to you,
that even if you became the best of women, I couldn't
like you again
nor can I stop loving you, no matter what you do.

53–85

I LOVE her and hate her at the same time.
How is that possible? I don't know.
It just is, and it nails me,
hurting and helpless
like a crucified slave.

54–87

NO WOMAN can ever really claim to be loved as much
as I love you, Lesbia,
no covenant was ever kept with such unwavering truth,
as I have shown, faithful to your love.

55-76

IF A MAN can take pleasure remembering the good he's
done, knowing he was true, that he was worth
trusting, that he never swore by a god's name so
people would believe his lies,
then, Catullus, you've stored up joy enough for the rest
of your life by the way you always kept honest faith
with that ingrate. All the good one person could say or
do to another—you did. You trusted her. It all came
to nothing.
Why keep tormenting yourself? Stop, for a minute, if you
can't stop for good. It's not the gods against you.
It's *you.*
I know. But she was my forever woman. I can't just
forget her.
You've got to. It's your only chance. It must be done,
whether you can or not.
Gods! If you can feel compassion for man, if you ever
wait for the last possible moment to help—that time
is now.
See how I hurt. My life wasn't guilty. Save me from this
—sickness, this lifewasting disease.
Sick sluggishness numbs me to the bone, nothing gives
comfort or distraction.
I'm not asking for her to love me. I'm not asking for her
to be good—I know she can't.
I just want to live, to shake this, this—sickness. Help
me gods,
remember my prayers and faith.

56-107

When you get something you wished for but never
expected—it's really delightful, it refreshes the soul—
like when I got back my Lesbia—no lost money found
was ever so much a recovery.
Yes, I'd hoped—but never expected it.
She returned, because she wanted to. O holy day
that brought her back! Who's happier, luckier than me?

57-109

You say you want only love and pleasure everlastingly
between us—
Great gods, let her honestly promise this, and say it with
all heart's truth!
Let us keep an everlasting pact of holy friendship
life long.

Rivals for Lesbia

58-40

RAVIDUS, Ravidus, are you feeling all right? What is it
makes you rush into my poetical line of fire?
Did a slapdash invocation by you offend some god whose vengeance
consists in getting you riddled with bursts of satiric verse?
Is that any way to get famous? Would you be the hero
of a poem at any price?
Whoever falls for my girl, falls to my pen.

59-37

There's, a low dive nine shops down from the temple of Castor and Pollux
where a crowd hangs out who think they own the only dicks extant.
—That they're the only ones allowed to screw girls, that everyone else is a nerd.

Dimwits! Don't you know I've got enough schlong to gag two hundred like you?
Think about it. And afterward I'd scribble your tavernfront
with how I rate you as cocksuckers.

The girl who slipped from my arms
—I loved her. No-one will ever love a girl that much—
my hard-conquered lady now resorts to this dump.
All you splendid young aristocrats love her, and, I'm sorry to say,
so do all the grubby little streetcorner sultans who conduct their amours in alleyways.

But especially you, Egnatius, with your elegantly cut long fop's hair,
you son of Celtiberia, land famous only for its rabbits,
who, like your barbarian ancestors, believe a thick beard makes you lovely,
yes, and teeth that shine from being rinsed in your own piss.

60–39

EGNATIUS always has a smile, his teeth are sparkling white.
If he's at court to help in a friend's defense,
when the lawyer's making the jury sob,
he grins.

At a funeral, when the groans of the mourners rise with
 the crackling of the pyre,
and the widowed mother cries for her lost, only and
 devoted son—
Egnatius grins.

Whatever the place, whatever the case,
whatever he's up to, the fellow is smirking. It isn't
 very nice.
No, and it isn't refined or elegant or smart. It's *sick*.
Therefore, I feel I should warn you:
were you a slick Sabine or a witty Tiburian,
a thrifty Umbrian or a paunchy Etruscan gourmand,
a Lanuvian whose dark skin sets off his smile, a
 Transpadane like my ancestors,
or *anyone* who cleans his teeth decently—I still wouldn't
 wish this continual grinning.
There's nothing so awkward as misplaced mirth.

Now you're a Celtiberian. It's a well documented fact
    that in the regions of Celtiberia
the custom is to brush the teeth and rub the pink gums
    with one's own morning urine.
Thus, we can only conclude that the shine of your teeth
is an accurate indication of how much piss you've
    drunk.

61–78*b*

IT PAINS me
that a pure girl's chaste kisses
should taste the pollution of your pissdrinking lips.
You won't get away with it, Egnatius.
Fame will chatter about you like an old laundress
and all the passing centuries will pause to laugh at you.

62–79

This may refer to Lesbia's (her real name was Clodia) brother Publius Clodius Pulcer, as the first line "Lesbius est Pulcer . . ." suggests. Clodius spent a lot of his time in court, answering charges, and was often accused of incest.

LESBIUS is a pretty boy—who denies it?
His sister Lesbia rates him above Catullus and all
    Catullus's kin.
I'd concede that pretty Lesbius
is worth a hundred people like Catullus,
if Lesbius could show me three decent people
who'd be willing to kiss, in greeting, those well-known lips
    of his.

63–82

Quintius, if you'd like Catullus to be more grateful
to you than he is for his eyes—and there's no more
precious possession than sight—
don't steal from him the thing that's dearer to him
than vision.

64–100

The very flower of Veronese youth, Caelius and Quintius,
are withering away
for love of Aufilenus and his sister Aufilena respectively.
They've become like brothers since they started courting
in the same family.
Which one am I wishing success to? Caelius Rufus, you're
the one I favor,
you showed yourself an outstanding friend to me
when you decided not to rival me for Lesbia
at a time when mad love for her was melting my marrow.
Luck to you, and all success in your passion for the
fair Aufilenus.

65-77

Rufus, I trusted you, my worthless friend
(worthless as you are, you've cost me plenty),
you sneaked into my confidence—only to burn me alive
—to steal away everything I had that was good!
You stole her! Poisoner
of my life, you make friendship a disease.

66-69

You really shouldn't be surprised, Rufus, that no woman
lets you lie on her soft thighs,
not even if you corrupt her with new clothes or clear
delightful gems.
An unpleasant breath of rumor wafts about you like
an odor—
to the effect that a wild goat lives in the valley of
your armpit.
—Everyone's a little apprehensive.
A very ugly beast, the goat is,
no fashionable girl would sleep with one.
Therefore, you should either kill that implacable enemy
of noses,
or stop wondering why ladies run away.

67–71

You're well avenged on your rival, Rufus. Even as he shares the pleasures of your bed,
he also shares, wonderfully enough, all your problems as well.
Viz.: the goat in your armpit that charges out with nostril-flattening force,
and the gout that makes you limp for woe.
As often as they fuck, vengeance is yours.
She suffers from his stench, and the gout makes him scream.

68–59

Rufa, the carrot-haired girl from Bologna,
gives blowjobs to her little brother,
red-headed Rufus. You know who she is,
Menenius's wife, the one you always see
in the paupers' graveyard grabbing snacks
from food-offerings set on the pyres.
Whenever she chases a loaf rolling out
of the blaze, the unshaven slave who tends
those flames runs over and gives her a whack.

69–91

I NEVER even hoped I could trust you, Gellius,
with the object of my agonizing self-destructive love
because I supposed you were loyal, or imagined you could
hold yourself back from any filthy act.
I trusted you with her for whom I feel such great
devouring passion,
because I knew she wasn't your mother or your sister.

Even though we've been friends a long time, I'd never
have believed you'd find it as exciting
to violate my friendship as to outrage the taboo
on family sex.
But, apparently, it served. So great is your joy
in any, however faintly, evil act.

70–90

LET a Magus be born from the criminal coupling of
Gellius with his mother,
and let that child be educated in entrail divination
according to the Persian rite.
For, if it's true what they say about the Persians'
unholy religion,
a Magus can only be born of a mother and son.
Only thus will the gods accept his chanted praises
as the fatty guts melt away in the altar's flame.

71–89

GELLIUS is skinny—what do you expect
with a good mother in excellent health, a very lovely
sister, an obliging uncle, and any number of
female relatives,
can you really expect him to put on weight?
Although he isn't excited by anything that doesn't outrage
the laws of gods and men,
as things stand, he's getting so much—*exercise,*
it's no wonder he's thin.

72–74

GELLIUS heard his stern old uncle fulminating against the
laxness of the times—
how it was criminal to have a little fun—or even talk
about it.
To make sure *he* never came in for such a scolding,
Gellius porked his rigorous uncle's wife.
Voila! Uncle is Silence personified, a regular Harpocrates.
It all fell out as Gellius wished. Uncle wouldn't say a word
at this point,
not even if Gellius crammed his cock in uncle's mouth.

73–116

GELLIUS, I really planned on sending you those poems
by Callimachus, an appeal
to your scholarly nature, to win you over,
so you'd act nice.
I had a cease-fire in mind.

I was casting about for the ideal means
to gift you with those poems.
A waste of time, Gellius,
you wouldn't even listen.

Fair enough. But every arrow
of insult you send in my direction
vibrates in the wall (not even close!).

But every phrase I shoot at you
will gore and gut. You refused
the poems? Excellent.
Now take what you deserve.

74–88

WHAT does he mean, that Gellius, staying up all night,
all naked, with his mother and sister?
Are they afflicted with the itch? And, does scratching
help?
What's he about, that Gellius? He won't let his uncle be
a husband in peace.
Do you have any idea what wicked things he does?
Not world-encircling Ocean, Tethys, and all the
sea-nymphs
could wash him clean. He really couldn't take
sexcrime any further, even if he
bent over and gave himself blowjobs.

75–80

How can I, Gellius, understand why it is that your sweet
 rosy lips
shine whiter than newfallen snow
when you wake up in the morning, and when you rise
from your gentle siesta
in the day's long warm hours?

There may be some truth to the whispers
that you swallow hard-ons?
I think that's it. Poor Victor's prick
dangles exhausted, your lips are painted with
pearly serous goo.

76–58

CAELIUS, my Lesbia, that same Lesbia,
that famous Lesbia whom Catullus loved
better than himself, than all his own kin,
is now to be found in Rome's back alleys
sliding back the foreskins
of great-souled Remus's descendants.

77-11

Furius and Aurelius, you'd follow your Catullus
    anywhere:
to where the utmost shores of India re-echo the river
    Ocean thrashing its way around the disk of Earth,
to Hyrcania, to silken Arabia, to Scythia's frozen fields,
to the archer Parthian's home, to where the seven mouths
    of Nile shoot silty color into the Mediterranean,
or up the skyish Alps to look out over Gaul, the Rhine,
    the terrifying sea, and Britain out on the world's rim
(now they're mere memoranda of Caesar's conquering).
My friends, ready to adventure so far off with me, taking
    chances on the gods' good will,
I only ask you to ferry back a message, not very long or
    very nice, to my girl:
that I hope she's getting on well with her lovers she takes
    on three hundred at a time,
loving not one, but all the same milking their dicks on an
    assembly-line basis,
not caring about my love, like she used to, my love cut
    down (her fault),
like a flower at the edge of a meadow razed by the passing
    plough.

Juventius

❧

THE ancient Romans, like English aristocrats and Bulgarian peasants, took open and equal pleasure in handsome women and beautiful boys. Thus Catullus had no compunction about falling in love with Juventius—a remarkable youth. Fourteen-years-old, greedy, fickle, seductive, a total tart. The poet also spent much jealous energy trying to keep the lovely Juventius out of the hands of his friends Aurelius and Furius.

78-48

JUVENTIUS, if I had the chance to kiss your golden face
three hundred thousand times—it wouldn't be enough.
No, not if the harvest of kisses were richly dense
as the ripe ears of grain in the field.

79-99

WHILE you were playing, my honied Juventius, I stole a
little kiss—
deeplier sweet than ambrosia—
I didn't get off too easy. For more than an hour I was
nailed to the highest cross!
I apologized, I wept. Nothing softens the cruelty of boys
like you.
You gargled, rubbed your gums, wiped your mouth on
your sleeve and spat—
did you think you'd catch a disease from me as
though I were some fucked-out whore?
Even though your anger only made me love you more,
you hurt me every way you could think of
until that ambrosial kiss I filched
felt like the kiss of death.

If my painful love for you gets punished like that—
that's the last kiss I steal from you.

80–103

Silo is an old and respectable Roman name, and it is most unlikely that he was a pimp. There is reason to believe he may have been a relative of Juventius's—perhaps his guardian.

SILO, if you give me back the ten sesterces, I won't care
how furious and outraged you are.
Or, if you'd rather keep the money, then at least be polite.
A pimp in the ecstasies of moral indignation is more than
I can bear.

81–15

I'M ENTRUSTING my lover to your care, Aurelius. I ask
a modest favor:
if you ever longed for anything and wanted it kept pure
and chaste,
then watch over my boy, protect him.
I'm not concerned about the public, the crowd that
hurries around trying to make a living.
It's you I'm worried about. You and your dong, a menace
to boys in general. Good lads or rotten brats—
no-one's safe.
Have anyone you want, as much as you want—if you see
'em, grab 'em!
—with this one exception. That's *not* a lot to ask.
But, if infatuation and brainless lust should lead you to
commit (you bastard!) such a crime,
to wit, poaching my boy,
then savage Destiny will beat you down with grief
—(for adulterers are, by tradition, punished thus),
as your legs are wrenched wide apart and tied, your
backdoor open
for the executioner to cram with radishes and
wriggling fish.

82-21

Aurelius, you nasty little thing, put some clothes on or
something! You look like Hunger in an allegory.
And the way you ogle my boyfriend—a staring starvation.
You aren't subtle about it either. Wherever I look, there's
Aurelius! cracking jokes for the boy, hanging on his
every word.
Think you'll get into his pants?
You'll blow me first!
I'd almost be willing to look the other way,
but if the boy went off with a charity-case like you
could I be sure he'd have clothes and a roof overhead?
I wouldn't even mind if you went leching after him on a
full stomach. But the way you lick your lips—when
did you last eat?
It's *unpleasant*. Quit while you're ahead, Aurelius,
don't make me force-feed you.

83-24

JUVENTIUS, flower of all the young men
who were, are or will be,
I'd sooner have you give that man the wealth of Midas—
which he'd need to get himself out of debt—than let him make love to you!
He's a real nice guy, is he?
That real nice guy doesn't own two shirts and he uses a shopping bag for a suitcase.
Say what you like—a goddamn shopping bag!

84-23

FURIUS owns neither slave nor strongbox, he couldn't
host so much as a spider or a bedbug, his hearth
doesn't house a living coal.
But he certainly has a father, and a stepmother whose
teeth could crunch through flint.

You get on just fine, Furius, with your dad and his dried
stick of a wife.
No wonder—indigestion's no problem, you've nothing to
fear from fire,
your roof's not about to cave in, theft is impossible,
your death would make no inheritors—you're exempt
from every peril.

Isn't it great? Sun, cold and hunger have given you
bodies drier than horn.
You're free from sweat, saliva, mucus, phlegm—
and as if that were insufficiently spic and span,
your ass is clean as a salt-shaker.
You don't crap ten times in a year,
and when you do, it's harder than a bean or a pebble.
You could crush it in your hands and never stain a finger!
Don't belittle your blessings, Furius, enjoy what you have.
And quit pestering me for that loan—you're fortunate
enough already.

85–26

FURIUS is so poor, the bugs in his house
took out a second mortgage on the roach motel.

86–16

We may assume that, after being the heroes of the preceding poems, Furius and Aurelius decided to write a few verses against the Cat. They probably suggested that he was immodest—no doubt they asserted that he was not a nice person—and surely they poked fun at his poem about wanting all those kisses. Catullus's reply has become his best-remembered, if not best-loved, poem.

I FUCK your asses, I feed you my dick,
Aurelius (you love it) and cocksucking Furius.
You said that I lack modesty, basing your charge on a few
    little verses about a boy?
Of course a god-fearing poet has to lead an upright life—
    that's no reason his poems shouldn't live it up
—poems that are witty, elegant compositions, even if
    they are a bit unbuttoned,
even if they do scratch you where it always itches,
    even if they do get people steamed up—
—I don't mean just schoolboys, no, even big hairy studs,
real animals, guys who need both hands to lift their dicks.
You thought I was naughty for writing the poem about
    wanting a million kisses?
Well fuck you.

87–106

WHEN you see a pretty boy with a slave auctioneer,
the assumption is he wants to be sold.

88–81

OUT of the entire Roman people couldn't you find a
classier man to have a crush on, Juventius?
Only him, from the sickly town of Pisaurus—he's paler
than a gilded statue.
He charms you? You dare prefer *him* to me?
Dig yourself, kid. Wake up.

Bithynia

PERHAPS about the time the affair with Lesbia concluded, Catullus set out for Bithynia (modern Turkey) on the shores of the Black Sea. He left Rome out of disgust with his present life and love-life, and, probably, due to some pressure from kinsmen to "make something of himself? In Rome the state and the army were functionally synonymous, and serving on the staff of a provincial governor was a standard move toward political power for a wealthy young aristocrat. This bid for respectability and "success" was the only yuppie move Catullus ever made— equivalent, for us, to taking a job in a prestigious law firm.

89–51*a*

Catullus's farewell to his urban ease, on setting out for Bithynia

CATULLUS, you haven't got enough to do, you wouldn't
carry on like this if you had a job.
This is the kind of idleness that ruins kings and cities.

90–46

On leaving Bithynia after his year of service

AT LAST the mildwarm spring brings in some
nonfreezing weather,
now the stormskied equinox hushes into the past,
pleasuring breezes ride in from the west,
Catullus, it's time to leave the Troian terrain of
Asia Minor, these fields of Bithynia, the capital
city Nicaea set in rich farmland,
leave now, before the air heavies with heat.
Let's run down toward the great cities of the Aegean
coast: Pergamum, Ephesus, Troy, well see them all.
My mind's a little anxious with wanting to be off—
I stretch my legs, feel my own glad strength—
Goodbye! my friends who came out with me to make it
in the provinces,
we all set out from home together, but each of us takes
his own path back.

91–31

Sirmio, out in lake Benacus, a peninsula, not quite
    an island
—to me you're dearer than all the islands Neptune holds
in clear lakes or throughout the bare unending sea.
I'm gloating over you, Sirmio, I can't believe I'm really
    here, that I've seen the last of Bithynia!
There's nothing richer than to feel your entire mind
lighten, to unhook the clasp of all anxiety;
after paying out twelve months in work overseas I come
    back to my household gods,
I'll sleep in my old bed like I wished I could. That alone
    repays the whole horrendous year.
Sirmio, I return and you're more beautiful; lake Benacus
    sparkles and splashes like laughter.

92–4

Gods, I offer up my thanks in this votive model of the
yacht that brought me back safe from my service
in Bithynia.
My friends, she was quick! Oared or windsped, she could
have rushed right past any wood afloat.
I call to witness the whole route, down the Adriatic's
stormy coast, then, rounding Greece, through the
hazards of the Cycladic isles, going up past famous
Rhodes, through the Dardanelles into the savage Sea
of Marmora, bordered by Thrace,
and finally, up through the Bosporus, to the mountain
where this yacht once wore
leaves that hissed in the wind, and it looked down from
the summit on the fierce Black Sea, where it would
first dip oar,
and carry its master away, plunging ahead, on a run,
the breeze full from behind.
And whichever way the winds invited, it kept straight
course, over uncontrollable oceans, making no
desperate prayers for aid to gods on shore, not once
all the way from that most distant sea to this clear lake
by my villa.
But that's past. The yacht's stored away, gone into quiet
retirement.
With a votive model I dedicate its soul
to you, the twin gods, Castor and Pollux, calmers of
storms.

93-10

I WAS up to nothing much. My friend Varus caught sight
of me and dragged me off to see his new girl.
So I saw her. You know, the little slut wasn't bad looking.
In fact she had a lot of class.
On the way Varus and I had been chatting about this and
that, how was Bithynia? did I make any money?
I leveled with him. Nothing there, for governors or
their staffs.
Especially when the governor's a cocksucker who could
care less what happens to them.
"Well, at least you got some litter-bearers? I mean,
that's where litter-bearing started."
I wanted (I admit) to impress the girl—
"Rotten as my province was, things weren't so bad I
couldn't find eight straight-backed slaves."
(Then or now I never had *one,* to so much as shoulder up
the leg-broken corner of my old bedstead.)
Then she, like a cunning little flirt, says,
"Oh *please,* Catullus, lend them to me for a while? I want
to go down to Serapis's temple."
"Hold on—just a moment—ah—*yeah,* I just
remembered—those slaves I mentioned—Cinna, ah,
Gaius Cinna—he just bought them—I still think of
them as mine, I mean, he lets me use them, and—"
"Tiresome girl! forget the details—go for the big picture."

94-9

VERANIUS, my best friend in the whole world, have you really come home to your household gods, your old mother, your brothers who love you?
You have. Great news! The best! You're safe, I'll see you, hear you telling all about Spain in that way you have, places, people, bits of history—
I hug you glad, I kiss your face, your eyes—who's happier, luckier than me?

95-28

DEAREST Veranius and my old friend Fabullus, provincial governor Piso's down and out staff, you guys sure travel light. I've seen refugees with better looking bundles.
Had enough of cold and hunger from that governor you thought you'd be plundering the province with?
Listen, when I followed *my* praetor for a year in the provinces all I got was fucked over. (Memmius, you found me lying on my belly, defenseless, and dorked me long and slow...) From the looks of things you got screwed by just as thick a prick.
People always tell you: "A man ought to cultivate friends among the nobility, try to get connections..."
May the gods pay them back, blueblooded creeps, disgracers of Romulus and Remus.

96–47

Porcius and Socration, Piso's hoods, fleas in the hair of the world,
that prick on legs gave you fat chances to bloodsuck the province—but not my friends Veranius and sweet Fabullus.
You'd get out of bed and slump half-awake to the next royal feast—my buddies had to hunt for dinner invites.

Brother Death

ALMOST the whole chronology of Catullus's life is guesswork, but my feeling is that his brother died about the time the affair with Lesbia was ending, and before Bithynia. It is possible that the first poem in this section (97–101) was written at Troy, on the way to or back from Bithynia. The others were composed at Verona, where Catullus withdrew from Rome and Lesbia on hearing of his brother's death.

97–101

GRIEF reached across the world to get me,
sadness carries me across seas and countries
to your grave, my brother,

to offer the only gift I still can give you—
words you will not hear.

Fortune has taken you from me. You.
No reason, nothing fair.
I didn't deserve losing you.

Now, in the silence since,
as is the ancient custom of our people,
I say the mourner's prayer,
do the final kindness.

Accept and understand it, brother.
My head aches from crying.
Forever, goodbye.

98-65

THOUGH heart's hurt exhausts me always now, and I
cannot enjoy
the company of those learned girls, the Muses,
or sweetly bring to birth a verse—
Terrible things have happened, my mind
hovers, incapable, in shock—

My brother just crossed the river Lethe, that coldest
stream of all's
washed his pale feet. Yanked out of sight
—engulfed by earth,
Trojan soil heaped heavy over him on the shore of
Rhoetum.

Brother, I loved you more than life, I'll never see you
now. Always I'll love you,
always sing sadder because of your death,
songs like those the nightingale sings, perched in thickest
treeshade, weeping her lost love.

Even though I grieve, Ortalus, I send you these poems of
Callimachus,
wrung from the Greek into Latin for you,

lest you think your wishes have vanished from my mind
like words in the wind, forgotten
like that apple (a lover's secret gift)
the girl in the story hid in a soft fold of clothing—
        when her mother came in
she stood up, it fell out, shot headlong across the floor
while a guilty blush overspread
her sad face.

99–68*a*

IT MEANS a lot to me that you sent me that letter,
opening your heart to me like that—
bad luck, sad accidents, tears—the whole shipwreck of your life.
It's as if I found you thrown ashore, unconscious in the foam,
as if I *could* rescue, drag you out of the grave.
The memory of love won't let you rest, sleep, the only comfort of the wretched,
calm sleep leaves you, alone, in a widower's bed.
The Muses can't divert you with deep sweet songs of the ancient writers,
you stay awake all night, jumpy and fretful,
I'm glad you look to me as a friend, ask me for poems and consoling.

Don't think I'm sick of friendship and its duties—
I've been having my own share of disaster.
Understand that I'm drowned in bad luck too.
Don't ask me in my wretchedness for cheering gifts.

When I'd just turned sixteen and started wearing a grown-up's white toga, in my life's glad springtime,
I wrote merry poems aplenty. She knows this well,
the goddess who tempers our anxieties
with bitter sweetness. But my brother's death took away my taste for the game.

My brother, taken so woundingly away, with you all
    my pleasures were buried, my whole family died.
All happiness left with you. Your love kept me alive.
When you were lost, I couldn't write, nothing was fun
anymore. So, Allius, when you tell me that I'm disgraced
    at Verona, that all the wealthy young men are
    warming themselves in the bed I left—
It's no disgrace, Allius, it's just sad.

So, forgive me if I can't send you anything. Grief has
    taken all.
I can't messenger you the books—I only brought one with
    me from Rome—I spend all my time there, that's
    where my things are.
Don't think I'm being stingy.
Another time
when I have something to give, I'll send it along.

100–68*b*

I CANNOT keep silence, Muses, about how Manius helped
me—his kindness, the favors he did me.
I cannot refrain from speech.
Time runs away, forgetting what's behind it, but the
shadows won't cover my buddy Manius.
I will tell it to you, Muses, you tell others, and this page,
like an old woman, will gossip on eternally.
Not even death will end his fame, nor will that tiny
acrobat, the spider,
weave her frail rare nets over his forgotten name.

You know what anxiety twofold Venus—lady of pleasure
and pain—gifted me with, how she shattered me,
my mind could have outvolcanoed Aetna, I surpassed in
steam the hotsprings of Thermopylae,
my eyes never ceased to irrigate my cheeks.

Like a gleaming stream leaping from a mountaintop's
mossy rocks,
a stream that dives down headlong slopes to become
a brook
for the valley-people, a sweet cool comfort
to sweating bedraggled travelers
when the heavy heat of summer is splitting the dry soil,
thus was Manus's aid to me. Or it was like

an easy-breathing helpful wind
that saves the shipshaken crew
when they're lost and exhausted in whirling black sea,
and they pray to Castor and Pollux, calmers of storms.

He opened house and grounds to us, made them wide
with his welcome
to me, my lady, and our love.
My bright goddess stalked into the house, trod the
polished threshold,
her white feet glowed and her sandals sweetly creaked.

She was like lovedrunk Laodamia entering the house of
her new husband
Protesilaus, a home that could not last,
since they forgot to sacrifice—no holy bloodshed
won them peace with the lords of heaven.
(Virgin Rhamnusia, sacred Nemesis, avenger of impiety,
I call you to witness that I go along with nothing
rashly begun without the gods consent!)
Laodamia learned by the loss of her man
how much the altar thirsts for pious gore,
she learned how one can continue to live
when love's been torn away.
She had to loose and lose him from her arms
before two winters of long nights
had satisfied her hungry love.

The Fates had known how soon and surely they'd
 be parted
if Protesilaus went, a warrior, to Troy—
for this was the time when Helen's theft
called noblest Greeks to Trojan plains.
Troy! that damned and criminal city,
mass grave of Europe and Asia Minor,
Troy, that burned the corpses of heroes
and turned to ashes so much courage and worth,
Troy, my brother's killer, my brother, grabbed
from my arms, my sun put out!
When you died, our whole family became like the dead,
we buried life and pleasure with you.
Your love had made us live.

You couldn't be placed among family graves,
among familiar stones.
Hopedestroying Troy keeps you,
your grave is lost to us in far and foreign Troy,
where all the youth of Greece once rushed,
leaving their homes, many forever,
so Paris shouldn't sleep easily,
or joy in his kidnapped mistress.

And so you lost your husband, Laodamia, sweeter to you
 than life itself,
Love caught you in its oceanic whirl,
raised you to heaven just to throw you down to hell,

into black depression as abysmal deep
as the channel that drained the river Olbios
and dried the swampy rich Arcadian land.
(They say it was dug by Hercules, who cut away
    mountains to make it,
about the time when he shot unerring arrows
into the monsterbirds of Stymphalia,
the fifth of his labors when he served Eurystheus,
unworthy taskmaster to the son of Jove.
Hercules earned by these tremendous efforts
the right to walk the halls of heaven,
himself become a god,
and he married Hebe, goddess of youth.)
But your love was profounder than
that Herculean chasm, that vast
heroic land-draining trench,
the love that bowed your untamed neck
to the yoke of marriage.
Your love, greater than that of an old father
at the end of his life, for his one grandson,
born at last to his only child, a daughter,
a grandson who grows into manhood, whom the old man
    can finally name in his will,
giving him the ancestral wealth. Now that venerable man
can laugh at his kinsmen, who with shameless
greedy joy expected his death.
The grandson has scattered the vultures
who circled his white head.

And your devotion, Laodamia,
was greater than the dove's
(that animal emblem of loyal love),
the dove, which overjoys in its snowy mate
and pecks gentle kisses on its lover's beak,
more shameless than a woman in heat.
But you, Laodamia, outfrenzied them all
once you were united with your blondhaired man—

but little or nothing less than you in ardor
was my lady and my light,
who conferred herself on my lap.
Shining Cupid rushed around her
peeping at me over her shoulder
—I saw him flash by in his yellow robe.

But Catullus alone is not enough for her.
I'll endure my modest lady's occasional intrigues.
I won't, like a fool, get irritable.
Often enough Juno, greatest goddess in heaven,
has to swallow back her anger
at her husband's unending affairs
—but it isn't right a man compare himself to gods.

Anyhow, her kinsmen never offered her to me
in marriage, saying: "Take her, and spare her father,
who trembles with age, the undelightful task of
supporting her." She wasn't led to me

by a parent's hand, into a house adorned
for the wedding, where Assyrian incense
spicily reeked.

She did give me amazing little favors
by night, gifts stolen from her husband's lap
—it's enough for me that she values
the time she sets aside for me.

I give you then, Manius, this poem as a gift,
in return for your many kind services to me,
so the coarse moss won't ever cover your name,
not today, tomorrow, or in the coming years.
And may the gods heap on in addition
those favors which Themis, goddess of Justice,
traditionally gives to loyal men.
Be happy, you and the woman who's all to you,
may your house last! Where my mistress and I played,
may Aufer always be well, at whose house I met her,
origin of all good things for me,
and above all, she who is dearer to me
than every other, dearer to me than my own being,
my lady, my light,
whose existence makes me wish to live.

Politics

In Catullus's time the Roman state was exploding—the system of government developed for a small city had survived into Rome's accession to empire—with predictable results. Every segment of society—slaves, plebians, equestrians, and nobles—was lashing out, not only for its due but for whatever it could get. Real power was held by men with military forces—Caesar, Pompey, and Crassus—who put through needed reforms only as a means of gaining popular support.

Catullus was an aristocrat with very little interest in politics. He wrote against Caesar, not out of conscience but because he found Caesar's generous, kingly manner irritating.

101–FRAGMENT 3

...No ONE escapes my lines...

102–57

THEY get on fine, those filthy faggots, Mamurra and
Miss Julius Caesar,
—not surprisingly,
one's disgraced in the provinces, the other's the shame
of the city.
Both of them fucked out and used up, you'd think they
were twins—they must have been roomies at the same
prep school.
Co-supremes and stars of adultery. Oh, they get on great,
that pair of poofs.

103–93

CAESAR? Caesar who?

104-29

ONLY a money-mad casino whore
could watch without comment Caesar's highliving
Lieutenant
Mamurra carting home the loot from aboriginal Britain
and savage longhaired Gaul.
Caesar, you faggot Romulus, you let him!
Then this loudmouthed *arriviste,* this strutting moneybag
rolls out a carpet of cash and strolls into everyone else's
bedroom
like an overgrown stupid Cupid.

Caesar, your homoship, fearless leader
Did you march our legions to the edge of the world
so this worn-out human dildo
would have more millions to piss away? That was mistaken
generosity.
Wasn't it enough he wasted his patrimony and the royal
treasure
you and Pompey brought back from defeated Mithridates,
then drained rivers of gold from the veins of Spain?
Now Britain and Gaul are on his menu?

Why nurture this sickness that eats away the healthiest
inheritance?
Was it to fill Mamurra's purse you bargained to divvy up
Rome,
for this you sealed that deal by marrying your daughter off
to Pompey (who's twice her age),
for this you wrecked the Republic?

105–43

GREETINGS, young lady whose nose is not the smallest,
whose feet could be prettier, whose eyes might perhaps
    be brighter,
whose fingers could have been longer, whose mouth drier,
whose vocabulary could stand a little refinement,
in short—the girlfriend of that sad little rake Mamurra.

Maybe out in the provinces you pass for pretty,
maybe the fond lieutenant M. would like to suppose
    you're competition for Lesbia,
but then his whole generation is famous for being stupid
    and tasteless.

106–41

AMEANA, that unprotesting young lady, hit me up for a
    hefty loan,
you know her, the girlfriend of that bankrupt playboy
    Mamurra of Formiae, the girl with the shapeless little
    nose?
Someone should inform her relatives, call her friends.
    The girl has delusions: she thinks I've got money
    to lend, that she can get loans on her looks!
Bring a doctor. Bring a mirror.

107–114

MAMURRA, the dick-faced lord of Firmum
is considered rich—and justly.
What nice things he has!
Fowl, fish, meadow and farmland, game—
his estate has everything. Yet all is not
enough—he still outspends it,
richly poor, splendidly destitute.

108–15

MAMURRA the Penis actually owns about thirty acres of
meadow, forty of arable, and the rest is swamp.
But people think he's richer than Croesus, that his
holdings (in a single leap) take in everything from
here to Hyperborea
and only the river Ocean abridges his uninterrupted run
of fields, farms, giant forests, and fishponds.
Well, that's a tall tale to be sure. But he himself is far
more amazing
—the very idea of a Penis owning real estate!

109–94

DICK-FACE fools around with a lot of ladies,
no-one's a whore-hound if not penis-brain Mamurra—
what's in a name? Everything.

110–105

Mamurra publishes some verses against Catullus . . .

A PENIS once tried to climb the sacred hill of Pieria
—the Muses, armed with pitchforks,
hurled him headfirst down.

111-54

Otho's head is really small, Hirrus has the unwashed legs
of a peasant,
Libo tends to fart, but quietly—
Even you, Caesar, and old Fufidius who warms his thin
cool blood with crime,
even you would have to admit that, on these particular
points, your friends are less than pleasant.
It's got nothing to do with politics—I'm only stating some
visible, physical facts.
You shouldn't be angry this time, O sole and only leader,
Caesar,
if my verses are hurtful, it's only through innocent
honesty.

112–84

Arrius was probably Quintus Arrius, a lowborn provincial who became something of an orator, serving as a stooge for the triumvir Crassus. Apparently he was the only one to protest the Lex Pompeia of 52 B.C.—which limited the length of speeches in court.

ARRIUS complained it was so "dock" out he didn't know
 how he could "pock" his chariot—
convinced he was speaking wondrous well, shouting out
 the words for added clarity.
That's how his mother, his freedman uncle, his maternal
 grandfather and granny spoke.
When he was sent to Syria we took off our earmuffs,
we heard other people pronouncing his favorite words
soft and smooth, we almost forgot to cringe.
But terrible news has reached us—he's on his way back—
if his ear-pierced shipmates don't throw him to
 the "shocks."

113-52

WHAT are you waiting for, Catullus? Surely it's time
to die.
Caesar's boy Nonius—that pimple—has risen on a
magistrate's ivory chair,
And Vatinius, another Caesarian pet, is worse by a
consulship—he actually got elected!
Why wait, Catullus? This is a good day to die.

Mythological Poetry

113–52

Boys:

Young women, all together, stand.
Evening's here. The star we've been awaiting,
the evening star rises white
from behind Olympus. Time for us
to leave the tables densely spread
with good rich food. The bride arrives.
Time for wedding song! Be present here,
Hymen, Hymen,
Hymen, Hymen, Hymen!

Girls:

There are the young men. Unmarried girls,
it's time for us to stand and face them.
The night-guiding star must have already passed
into Thessaly, invading our horizon.
That's it—what else would make them
so leap up? But, quick as they are,
reckless they aren't.
Their song will beat ours.

Boys:

Friends, this won't be an easy victory,
those virgins have their song by heart,
and words worth remembering. That's no surprise,
they worked with total attentive mind.

Even when we practiced, we were thinking
of other things. We deserve to lose.
Victory loves painstaking care.
Pay attention *now* at least—they're starting
and, ready or not, well have to chant
something in reply.

Girls:

Evening star, cruelest glitter
in all the sparkling sky,
who pull the girl from her mother's arms,
reaching back even as she's led away,
you give a chaste girl to cool a young man's burning.
When a city's sacked, can the enemy
do anything worse?

Boys:

Evening star, merriest spangle
in all the scintillating sky,
whose fire ratifies marriage pacts,
the promises made by parents and men.
None can be joined, Hesperus,
until you flash assent.
What god's gift is more wished for
than this glad tick of time?

Girls:

Hesperus has kidnapped another from among us,
Hesperus, who starts the watchman's rounds.

Night hides the thief, who, as Hesperus
you lead in, then, with change of name,
as Lucifer, the morning star,
your glimmer winks on the thief as he leaves.

Boys:

Hesperus, virgins complain about you
in play. Their mourning's make-believe.
Their carping's a cover for stronger
unspoken desires,
O Hymen, wedding god!

Girls:

A flower born alone behind garden walls,
a stranger to browsing herds,
never torn out by a passing plough,
gently petted by breezes, encouraged
by suns, raised by rainfall—
many girls want such a flower,
many boys as well. But, picked,
it withers young and no one
wants it, girl or boy.
A virgin's loved so long as she's
untouched. Once her chaste flower's plucked,
her body's all polluted, she becomes
an unpleasantness, avoided by girls
and shunned by boys.

Boys:

An unwed vine grown in bare field
never rises, never swells mellow ripe grapes.
It sends weak shoots at random low
along the ground, top and root
together, directionless. No farmer ever
looks after it. Likewise, a virgin,
never made a woman, gets nothing but old.
But the vine that's married to a tree
is tended, bulls plough by to benefit
her, the farmers guardian her.
So, a virgin worthily paired
at the right time's a joy to her husband,
no burden to her kin.

Girl, don't struggle against the match,
you have no right. Your own father gave you,
mother too. You must obey.
Your virginity's not yours alone—
a third's your father's, your mother owns a third,
and only a third is yours.
It's two against one. Majority rules.
They gave the groom their rights to you
together with the dowry.
O Hymen, marriage god!

115–FRAGMENTS 1 & 2

Priapus, child of Venus and Bacchus, hero of 115–fr. 1 & 2, a pot-bellied garden-gnome with an oversize prick—sort of like a teapot—represents a universal idea, the scarecrow/fertility god. Under this name he was first worshiped on the Hellespontic coast of Greece, and there chiefly at Lampsacus, the only city to give him founder's honors by stamping his image on the coinage.

From there his worship spread. Priapus traveled east in Alexander's train, winning hearts for Hellenism. Alexandria became his metropolitan see, where he was celebrated with poetry and public worship. From there he traveled to Rome, where, by the time of Augustus, no garden was elegant without him.

Catullus is credited with several Priapeia, the numbers 18–20 deleted from modern editions and now to be found among the Vergilian apocrypha, as well as this authenticated fragment.

I DEDICATE and consecrate these words to you,
    Priapus, founder of Lampsacus,
whose shores are richer in oysters
than all the rest of the Hellespontic coast...

...I'd like to try it and see...

116-64

THEY say Mount Pelion's topmost pines
once swam the great sea's fluent waves
when the chosen, toughest young men of Greece,
hoping they could steal the golden fleece,
dared go the ocean in a quick ship,
raking the darkblue waterplains with firtree oars.

For them the goddess who holds the Acropolis
hilltopping high Athens herself invented that waterchariot
zooming on the lightest breeze. She assembled
the piney woodwork of the curving keel.
The speed of that first ship was education
to Amphitrite—then still a naive
young brine-goddess.
Pallas built that yacht whose beakish prow
ploughed up the plains of windy sea—
the waters wrenched by oarage foamed white and
    spit glitter.
Suddenly nymphs of the waves raised their faces
clear of the twinkling flood,
surprised by *this* seamonster.
Then and only then did mortals see by daylight
the daughters of Nereus all naked, standing
up to their breasts in the whirling silver.

Then, they say, Peleus ignited
with love for Thetis, who, for her part,
didn't scorn a mortal marriage. Even her father
judged they should join.

Heroes, born in that most desirable time of all the ages,
my chants will summon up all of you
often, and especially you, uniquely greatened
by the blaze of your wedding torches, allfortunate Peleus.
Jupiter'd wanted Thetis for himself, but the father of
  the gods
yielded her to you, defender of Thessaly.
Thetis accepted you, Tethys and Oceanus,
who include the whole disk of earth in a fluid embrace,
let you lead their granddaughter away.

The wanted time came, all Thessaly crowded
the house, the palace was choked with partying
joyfaced people holding out gifts. The town of Cierum
was derelict, they evacuated the vale of Tempe,
the homes of Crannon, Larissa's walls,
everyone came to pack Pharsalus.

No farming got done, no curved rakes lopped
the ground clear of lowtrailing vines, no bull
pulled gouging plough downfield, tearing up the soil
  in clods.
No pruning hook thinned treeshade,
ploughshares left lying roughened with rust.

But the glorious chambers of Peleus's residence
silverflashed and goldglared. Every door opened
on a vista of room after rich room receding
into magnificent distance. Throney chairs
glittered white ivory, goblets splashed reflected light
across altarly tables. Glistening
with royal treasure, the whole house joyed. Amid
    the seats,
the sacred marriage-couch of the goddess,
shaped and smoothed from Indian tusk,
draped with fabric saturate in richest red
then tapestried over with joltingly skillful
images of heroes.

You could see Ariadne on the shore of Naxos,
in the tideline's watery noise,
staring out after Theseus, who falls away
into a vanish, ferried out of sight
by no slow boat. She stands there, madness
building up inside her, not believing
she's really seeing this—she's just then waking
up from her cheating sleep, and starting
to comprehend that she's been ditched,
left sorrowsick on the blank unpeopled sand.

The young man of memory conveniently weak
fled, his oars beating back the waves, his meaningless
promises blown in the storm, words in the wind.

The daughter of royal Minos, standing in the seaweed,
looks out after him with sad sweet eyes,
staring, rigid, looking like that famous
statue of the Bacchante stunned by the god.

The seabreeze doffs her gauzy turban,
her dress falls delicate down from shoulder,
frees her firm little breasts,
then everything slips from her body, and the waves roll up
to touch.

Poor girl, Venus made you crazy with nonstop tortures
of love.
Ever since Theseus left the sweep of his home shores
and came to a harsh king's Crete.

A godsent plague had made Athens agree
to pay for having killed a Cretan prince.
They sent a yearly gift of boys and girls
to be Minotaur's dinner. Athens's walls narrowed
on the people so sadly harassed.
Then Theseus chanced his own adventurous body
so his friends wouldn't have a monster's belch
for a funeral oration. He pushed off in a light boat
on a gentle wind, came to tyrant Minos's castle.

Fourteen-years-old, perfumey and warm
from her mother's lap, the royal daughter saw him

and her eyebeams lit. Before she could look down
or turn away, Love seared into her
like a branding iron. The damned, the holy
Thief of Hearts, who mingles our anxieties
with joy, made her moan under her breath
and shiver for the yellowhaired stranger.
And she paled like the gleam on gold
when she learned hed come courting glory or death
from her brother the monster.

Silent prayers and promises rose
from her lips to the gods like incense
—sweet and useless. Nothing could stop
the hero's and the Minotaur's collision.
And the Minotaur fell, like a widebranching oak
or a pitchsweating pine atop Mount Taurus,
twisted back and ripped out in the whoosh
of a stormwind spinning insane;
all its wooden roots yanked from the ground,
it crashes headlong, busting up forest
and snapping off boughs far around. Thus Theseus
decked that bullbrowed psychopath, beat
that huge brutal body down, goring only
air with its horns. The hero turned back,
big with glory, through the Labyrinth's
mixed-up paths unerrored on the trail of thread he'd left.

Then Ariadne shipped with him to Naxos's wave-sprayed
shore,
but he did a quick dissolve the second sleep put out
her lights.
Many times in heart's madness she emptied her chest
in clear loud calls and cries. She climbed
the steep rough mountains to plunge her gaze
over the open sea's flowing tremendous desert,
then she ran down and right out into it,
holding up her fine soft skirts. The slapping waves
softly burst brine against her knees. Wetfaced with tears,
gasping out cold sobs, she told it:

"You took me away from my father, my house,
the altars of my gods, just so you could lose me
on the first empty shore? I believed your fawning voice,
I doomed my brother by helping you.

"Did a lioness in labor drop you in the desert?
Did the sea spit you up? Did you swim up into existence
from a pool of quicksand? This is how you pay back
the rescue of your life?

"At least you could have taken me with you,
I'd have been a happy slave to wash your feet,
only to make up your purplequilted bed.

Now you're out in mid-ocean, I'm on the beachhead
of nowhere.
I wish you'd never come to Crete, bringing the bull
terrible tribute. I'm oceaned off from everyone.
If I could leave now, *would* I go home—
to be the guest of honor at my brother's funeral?
Maybe follow my lover now bending his ship's tough
oars against the ocean to get away from me?

"Furies, snakehaired punishers of men, bring my pain
to him!"

She said. Jove heard. The universe nodded assent,
disheveling sea, lurching earth, flickering all the stars.
Then Theseus forgot the glad flag hed promised his father.

Before yielding Theseus to negotiate winds
on the godbuilt ship, his royal father said:

"My son, whom I meet for the first time only now when
I'm already old,
do I have to risk never seeing you again, do you have
to try this adventure?
My luck and your courage have joined to rob me of you—
my eyes are still hungry for the sight of your face.
I cannot gladly let you go, I'll rub dirt and dust in my
hair for a mourning
and hang black sails on the boat that takes you from me.

"Athena help you butcher the bull! Remember, when you
see the home hills,
show you're safe. Raise white sails."

But Theseus's promise left him like a blown cloud quits
a mountaintop.
His father looked, saw dark sails, jumped the cliff
of despair.
Brave Theseus was home for the funeral, the daughter of
Minos avenged.

But even then Bacchus was coming with Silenus and the
pack of satyrs,
Bacchus came for you, Ariadne, in love with you!
Running insane, the bacchantes turned heads and howled,
waved wands and bloody limbs of cows torn up alive.
Some held in baskets the cult's secret emblems—which the
uninitiate would love to hear about—
they thumped their drums, blew hoarse buzzing trumpets,
raised a delicate jingle of brassy chimes,
while barbarian flutes shrilled sweet horrible tunes.

—That was the splendor of the tapestry covering the
goddess's welldressed couch.
When the Thessaly-folk had gorged their eyes on it,
they left to make room
for the holy gods.

Just as the breath of morning gently ruffles an
easylying sea
and pushes along the sloping waves
with sound of little wet rippleslaps,
then the waves rise with the rising dawn wind, and enlarge
into big swimming billows, glimmering
back the sky's red light—so
the guests rose one by one then altogether up,
flowing out with backward glances
at the shining godfilled palace.

Them gone, Chiron arrived from Peleus's top with
woodgrown gifts,
garlands plaiting together all flowers of mountain, field,
and riverbank,
woven into long floral cables, they hung along the walls
painting a perfume landscape on the palace air.
From Tempe where branches sway in sky and nymphs
dance the earth
came Peneus, bringing whole rooted trees, high beeches,
noble straighttrunked laurels,
nodding planes, flexible poplars and skyish cypresses
to forest the city and cool the palace in soft green shade.

Prometheus came, still wearing thin scars that showed him
once immortally tortured.

Allfather came with his entire divine household,
leaving only the sun behind in heaven.
While the gods and heroes feasted, the Fates were there,
 busy,
trembly hands plucking at their everlasting work,
drawing soft wool from distaff, rolling it into a thread
 between their fingers,
nipping off stray fibers with their teeth, winding it onto
 the spindle.
The Weird Sisters working sang this song, and wove their
 words into reality.

"Hear now the Fatesong, Peleus and Thetis, we true sisters
 foretell you good marriage,
and sweet exhausted lovesleep with Thetis's smooth arm
 around Peleus's thickmuscled neck.
A marriage-pact of lasting peace, a son, Achilles, powerful
 runner,
enemytamer! Old Trojan mothers
will name him Death
as they bruise their own flabby flesh
and tear their whitehair beside their children's pyres.
Because of your son, Achilles, beautiful hero spattered
 with gore,
plougher of men in Troyfield.
He'll clog the Scamander river with bodies, warm that big
 stream with seepage of red.

When battleglad Achilles dies, they'll splash his tomb with
hot girlblood.
Polyxena, the captured Trojan princess, will have her neck
pulled back and slit like a heifer's.
They'll wave her head to the crowd while her trunk
falls flat.
Hear us Peleus, live and love,
we promise the sea-nymph Thetis will bear you
Achilles, a godlike son."

So the Fates sang before Peleus. In those times, before
religion became a joke,
the gods would visit the homes of great men.
On festival days, when a hundred bulls fell heavy
to earth, Zeus's temple flashed with the present god.
Bacchus would herd his wildhaired screamers
to cities where his altars sweetly reeked
—and the glad inhabitants ran out to meet him.
Mars, Athena, and Nemesis would warcry across the sky
over battle's clang.
But since criminals have polluted the earth, and big
bucks buy justice,
since brothers' hands are sticky with brothers' blood,
since lunatics make our lawless laws, the gods no longer
show themselves to us,
they don't want to be seen with our kind.

117–66

Catullus's Latin translation of a lost poem by Callimachus

THE king asked angrily: "Who dares to rob
the gods and mock the monarch? Terror held
the court in awed if awkward quietude.
"Who snitched the lock of hair my royal wife
Berenice deposited in Venus's shrine—
a thankful offering for my return
from devastating all Assyria?"
Then Conon spoke, the court astrologer:

Conon, who'd considered every light throughout the
whole tremendous heavens,
what hour each is reborn in the blue, what time it dies
from sight,
when the sun's white blasts of heat will muffle under
eclipse,
why the stars move in obedience to Time,
how gentle love called the moon down from her
skyish ride
to set upon Endymion, the sleepy shepherd boy,

—that heavenly scholar, Conon, spoke, and thus appeased
the king:

"That lock of hair, once Berenice's, now hangs among
the stars,
placed there by the gods!"

Meanwhile the sad if stellar bangs lamented in the
heavens:

"I am those curls Berenice vowed the gods, as she
outstretched her smooth arms in prayer,
when the king, enhanced by marrying her, went off to
devastate Assyra,
still spattered with the traces of that bloody bedtime
scuffle
in which he carried off the queen's virginity.

"Do brides really dread the wedding night, do they really
want to cheat their parents out of grandsons?
So they irrigate the bedsheets with their phoney tears
—so help me all the gods, their groans are faked.

"I learned that from the queen's unending complaints
—how she grudged entrusting her man to battle!
Does she claim it wasn't the empty bed she feared—
she only wept because he was her cousin?

"I suppose, Berenice, it was only family feeling that made
you so grief-weak you couldn't walk or speak?

"From the vantage-point of your own head I've seen your
 courage,
from earliest girlhood. I remember (if you don't) how
 you slew
the man you were engaged to, so you could marry
 this king.
The tragic speeches you made the day he left! By Jupiter,
 how often you wiped your eyes!
What god was it transformed your supposed coldness?
What other god than Love?

"The king left. To ensure his return, you sacrificed a
 bull
and vowed my fuzzy self to the gods. When he
 came back,
having added Asia Minor, as far as the Euphrates,
 to Egypt,
she kept her word and I became a tuft twice removed—
first to the temple, then wafted to the skies—

"Against my will, O queen! I swear it by your head!
 A curse upon me
if I lie. But who can stand up to metal?
The greatest mountain the sun rises over, Athos itself,
 yielded to steel
When Xerxes cut a ship canal through the isthmus and
 sent his goyish fleet swimming through the slopes.

When such give way to forged tools, what hope for me
who am mere filament?
Jupiter! May the whole race of Chalybes perish, that
Black Sea tribe, to whom it first occurred
to disembowel their mother earth and scrape the ore from
her ribs of rock, to shape the cruel metals!

"My hairy sisters wept for me, cut off from them forever,
then Emathion, son of the Dawn, appeared, in the form
of an ostrich, raising a wind at each nod of his
stubby wings
—the servant of Venus—he flew me up the night sky, and
placed me in Aphrodite's holy lap.
(By luck the Love goddess was vacationing in Egypt at
the time.)
She, lest the crown of Ariadne shine in the sky without
competition,
she made me gleam there too, soggy with tears, kidnapped
from the head of blonde Berenice,
a new constellation among the old, I float over by the
Great bear, Callisto, between the lights of Virgo and
bad-tempered Leo.
I sink nightly down the skies, leading stupid Bootes—
better known as the little bear—who can hardly find
his way
to the ocean to set. He always gets there late.

"Though at night I get to hear the footsteps of gods above
me, day sinks me in the gray sea again.
Nemesis, let me speak this out unpunished—I don't lack
reverence for the starry company
I'm forced to keep—but all the same
no coward fear will make me hide the truth,
though all the stars should sing together "O, come off it,
girl!"
Nothing will prevent me from opening my honest heart
like a book, that all may read—
all this superlunary stuff doesn't divert me. It's torture to
be exiled, forever, I presume,
from the dearest head of all, where I fed deliciously
on pleasantly fragrant moisturizing shampoos, mild
cleansers and rich conditioners
imparting body, bounce and luster!

"You girls, whom the long-awaited wedding day has
joined, by torchlight, to your true soulmates,
don't unbutton, setting forth your sweet little titties,
before you offer up in my honor an alabaster box full of
choicest haircare products,
you chaste obedient maidens! But girls who sleep
around—
let dirt drink in their spilt gifts—I reject them!
I don't need any favors from unworthy hearts.
But, pure new brides, may harmony always modulate the
measure of your wedded lives.

You, my queen, when you stare at the stars and light
    lamps in honor of Venus—
don't let me dry out up here in the breezy ether,
pour out pomades for my frazzled sake.
—I wish the stars would fall! I want to be hair again!
    Let Aquarius glare by Orion in my place."

118–63

Cybele, the Great Mother, is an earthfertility goddess from Asia Minor with a dead and resurrected consort named Attis. Cybele's cult was, on the Sibyl's advice, imported to Rome in 205 B.C., as a strategic deity during the wars with Hannibal. She ingratiated herself with the Romans by ensuring that Scipio defeated Hannibal at Zama that same year. Henceforth her cult was maintained in a sacred cloister on the Palatine, and carefully sequestered, as the Romans were disgusted to learn that their latest goddess delighted in wild parties run by eunuch priests.

Little more is known about Cybele than can be deduced from this poem.

A FASTMOVING cruiser shot over deep seas
carrying Attis from Greece to Asia Minor.
He landed, ran through the Trojan groves
into the forest-shadow-world of the goddess.

Angry madness revved his head like an engine—
it didn't seem real when he struck down with sharp flint
and lopped away the weight between his legs.
His whole body weakened, feeling
the last of his manhood drain hot down his legs,
bloodspattering the ground.
Then he/she grabbed the light tambourine that thumps
 out a summons
to your sacred rites, Cybele, Great Mother!

Battering the tight bullhide with soft fingertips,
it shivered and started singing to the others:
"You eunuchs, you priestesses of Cybele,
to the high groves—go! you straying cattle,
Cybele's, the Lady of Mount Dyndymus's herd.
Like exiles you couldn't wait to leave,
you followed my lead over violent sea,
you unsexed yourselves,
like me, you made yourselves women
and showed your hatred of women's love.
Dance! Our mistress laughs to see us crazed!
To Cybele, run, run, to the groves of the goddess,
where cymbal screams in a metal voice, drum
 bellows back,
where heavy Phrygian flute buzzes through its
 curving pipes,
where ivycrowned Maenads dance,
slavering, snapping in convulsions
electrifying the holy mysteries with loud shrill howls.
Go mad!" sang Attis, the unwoman.

Their tongues flickered out as they yowled the cry
 of Bacchus,
the smooth drum hollow thudding replied,
rattling cymbals clattered shrill,
the whole chorus ran up Mount Ida, gasping,
chaos on a hundred feet. Attis with his drum
in the lead, like an untamed bullock running away from
 the yoke,
and the Gallae, the sacred eunuchs, ran after.

When they reached the home of Cybele, exhausted,
they fell asleep, nor even thought of food.
Stupor shut their eyes in sinking weakness,
their madness gentled into peace.
When goldfaced sun turned on its beaming eye,
scanning bright white sky, hard ground, rough sea,
scattering night, sleep ran away
from waking Attis. (The Grace Pasithea,
bride of Sleep, eagerly lifted the drowse-god
into her trembling lap.)

Calm and sensitive, without the speeding madness now,
Attis begins to consider what she's done.
Her clear mind sees where she is, and without what,
she runs hysterical back to the shore,
eyes dropping tears into sea.

"My country, where I was born, country that gave me life,
I left you like a runaway slave—to come to Ida's
snowy forests of wild animals. I wander among their lairs.

"Where's home, where can I look for it?
The moment my madness goes
I find only forest. I lost my country,
possessions, friends, family. I lost the forum,
the wrestling matches, the racetrack, the gym.
My soul keeps asking for all I lost, looking for all
    that's gone.

"I had that noblest beauty—which is male.
As man, as adolescent and as boy
I was the star of the gymnasium,
muscles gleaming with oil, glorious, stared at,
garlands were hung on my house, would-be male lovers
    spent their nights in my doorway
—in the morning I had to step over their sleeping bodies.
Am I now the serving girl of the goddess, one of
    Cybele's slaves?
A maenad, a neuter, a piece of what I was?
Will I have to live on cold snowy Ida,
pass my life under Phrygia's tall pillars,
living with deer and wild boar?

"Now I regret, now I feel my wound."

As these words passed his red lips, the goddess heard—
Cybele unyoked her chariot's lions, flickered her whip
    along the sides of the left cow-killing beast:
"Go after him, teach him the madness, make him rave
    again—with fear!
Hunt him back to my grove—he thinks he can leave!
Roar, make the whole place tremble resonant,
go, heavy tail slamming against your own flanks,
red mane slapping thickmuscled neck."
Menacing Cybele spoke and loosed it,
the eager beast ran roaring off, crushing underbrush,

came to the wet whitefoaming shore, saw feeble Attis
　　by the oceanplain
and charged. She ran crazily back into the woods, a
　　serving girl
for the rest of her life.

Goddess, great goddess Cybele, Lady of
　　Mount Dyndymus,
may all your madness remain far from me—
inspire others, drive others mad.

119–61

YOUR mother was Urania, who holds the telescope and
chart of stars,
you live with the Muses on Helicon,
and it's you that bring tender girls to men, you carry
them off into marriage, Hymen.
Crown yourself with fragrant marjoram, put on the
full-length bridal veil,
come happy here, the yellow shoes on your pale feet,
all excited for the glad day, singing bridal anthems in a
bell-toned voice clear and high, dancing, stamping the
ground, waving your torch.

Here comes the bride, looking like Venus on her way to
the fatal beauty contest,
Junia Aurunculeia, lovely and well-omened for
Manlius Torquatus.
She glows like an asian myrtle whose branches shine with
flowers which the Hamadryads tend and water for
their own delight.
Come then, nymphs, leave your caves beneath Mount
Helicon cool with the mist from waterfalls, call
the lady here with music she's eager to hear.
Love crowns her mind as ivy wreathes itself around a tree.
Untouched virgins, you for whom a day like this is
coming soon, chant the rhythmic song for Hymen,
have him hurry to his work, to guide in Venus and
join these two in love.

Who in heaven's better worshiped here on earth
    than Hymen?
What god gets more requests from anxious lovers?
Old trembling parents invoke you for their children;
    virgins loose their dresses for you, let the cloth slide
    down their legs, and men are always nervous about
    you, for fear you'll come, for fear you won't.
You take a fourteen-year-old girl and give her to a rough
    young guy—in his arms I think she'll soon forget
    about her mother's lap.
Without your help love brings on gossip, with you families
    are made, and there are children who'll stand by their
    parents, citizens to guard the borders.

Throw back the doors, she's here. All at once the torches
    flare up, tossing back their flaming manes. She stops,
    embarrassed, hears the wedding song and her eyes
    brim. Easy, Vinia, there's no serious risk
of any girl on earth being prettier than you.
You look like a hyacinth standing out among the many
    flowers of a rich man's garden;
but the day wastes while you hesitate, come now, young
    bride, please hear our verses, look how the torches
    shake their manes of blonde fire. Forward, newly
    wedded girl!
Manlius isn't the sort to cheat on you. How could he
    sleep apart from your firm and beautiful breasts? Hugs
    and holdings will tie him to you, sure as vines embrace
    a tree, and so will the pleasures of the bed, while the
    night slips by and when you rest at noon.

Why wait? The time is now. Lift the torches, boys, he's here, I see the flare of his cape, louder, sing it rhythmic, Hymen, god of Marriage, Hymen, Wedding-god!

But don't leave out the teasing verses, the rude Fescennines!

Hear that, slave boy, master's bed-pet? throw the children their almonds now, your master's got another love. Give the kids their almonds, lazy creature! You've been a kid long enough—this marriage ends *your* vacation. Yesterday the village girls weren't good enough for you, now the barber shaves your peachfuzz, playmate! You can bet the groom's sorry to be giving up his smooth little boyfriend, but he will. Not that there's any harm in it, but marriage is marriage! Now bride, don't you refuse him what he wants, or you know hell go looking for it someplace else!

Your husband's house and family are powerful and rich. Accept them, let them wait on you all your life, till your trembling white head is nodding yes yes to everything.

Set your golden feet on the threshold, touch the polished door. Good luck enters with you. Your husband reclines on the purple couch, leaning toward you, watching, imminent. Both of you burn, one for the other, hearts beating deep and fast.

Boy, let go her arms, she goes to her man's bed. Good
    women, grown old with your husbands, set her there
    now. Come, husband, your wifes in bed for you, face
    glowing like a flower, a white daisy, a yellow poppy.
But by the gods you're beautiful as she. Venus is with
    you. Come on! Delay is the waste of a world.
And Venus help your open honest love!
Who could count your pleasures? Easier to number the
    sands of Africa, the sparkling stars.
Play now, have children soon. A great family should have
    descendants. I want to see a little boy in his mother's
    lap, his tiny lips half-parted in a newborn smile
stretching out his arms and laughing for his father. May
    the boy's face show the father's features and so the
    mothers virtue. Let the mother's reputation be proof
    of the boy's parentage
as Telemachus was honored in Penelope, the best, the
    only wife.

Girls, close the doors, enough play now. Good bride and
    groom, live happy, pass your youth in uninterrupted
    kindness.

120–34

UNDER Diana's protection, pure girls and virgin boys, we sing Diana, high powerful child of universal Jove, born beside an olive tree on Delos, huntress, lady of the mountains, lady of the moist fresh forest, lady of secret valleys and loud fast rivers.

Diana, whose name is Lucina, Lightbringer, who every month restores the vanished moon. Diana whose name is Juno-Lucina, who hears the pained prayers of birthing women. Diana, whose name is Proserpina—the crossroads her sacred place—nightgoddess, queen of underworld.

Threefold Diana, huntress, birth-helper, and Luna, shining with borrowed light, Diana, in your monthly circle measuring out the turning year, filling the farmer's rough-walled barn with fruit and produce, vegetables and grain.

Be you holy and exalted by whatever name will please you! And now, as of old, with your good power, protect the people of Romulus.

Concordance
Traditional - Rabinowitz

1-1	27-3	54-111
2-40	28-95	55-8
2*b*-42	29-104	56-18
3-44	30-27	57-102
4-92	31-91	58-76
5-39	32-23	58*b*-8
6-38	33-20	59-68
7-41	34-120	60-29
8-47	35-17	61-119
9-94	36-31	62-114
10-93	37-59	63-118
11-77	38-21	64-116
12-9	39-60	65-98
13-5	40-58	66-117
14-15	41-106	67-19
14*b*-2	42-34	68*a*-99
15-81	43-105	68*b*-100
16-86	44-24	69-66
17-7	45-30	70-48
18-omitted	46-90	71-67
19-omitted	47-96	72-46
20-omitted	48-78	73-28
21-82	49-6	74-72
22-16	50-12	75-52
23-84	51-45	76-55
24-83	51*a*-89	77-65
25-37	52-113	78-33
26-85	53-14	78*b*-61

79-62
80-75
82-88
83-63
84-112
85-53
86-43
87-54
88-74
89-70
90-70
91-69
92-103
93-103
94-109
95-32
96-32
97-22
98-11
99-79
100-4
101-97
102-4
103-80
104-50
105-110
106-87
107-56
108-26
109-57
110-35
111-36
112-10
113-25
114-107
115-108
116-73
fr. 3-101
fr. 1 & 2-115

www.ingramcontent.com/pod-product-compliance
Lightning Source LLC
LaVergne TN
LVHW051001080826
845145LV00009B/2397

* 9 7 8 0 8 8 2 1 4 1 5 1 0 *